THIS BOOK BELONGS TO

For Mary Frances

FRIENDS FOR ALL SEASONS

A Year In The Garden

Written and Published by Donagh Hourihan

ISBN 978 1 5272 9542 1

DonaghHourihan.com

On a cold and frosty morning under January's dark skies,
I heard a distant calling as the dawn began to rise.
It was a friendly blackbird singing out a mellow tune,
While resting by the hedgerow underneath a bright full moon.

The hard ol' frozen ground had kept the worms out of his reach.
Berries were in short supply, rationed to just two each.
I willed myself out of my bed and put my wellies on,
To see what seeds were left for him or if they were all gone.

Each footstep made a crunching sound as I trudged through the grass.
The torch light flickered on the ground with darkness slow to pass.
And looking up I saw three empty feeders in the light,
So off I went and filled them up while different birds took flight

As soon as I had gone inside,
the word was passed around.
Breakfast had just been served,
with birds now all inbound.

Finches, siskins, robins, tits, all queued up for their food.

But when the pesky magpies
came, it all got rather rude!

"Move it or lose it!"
"Retreat!"

February then came around and new flowers appeared.
Snowdrops popped up in the grass, the first ones of the year.
Crocuses and daffodils then followed close behind,
Welcoming the Springtime with their colours all combined.

Attracted by the vibrant hues, bees started to drop by.
Awoken from their slumber, they took off for the sky.
They danced around the flower beds and feasted all day long,
And hid beneath the petals when they heard a new bird's song.

Tulips rose up from the ground as March came rolling in,
While Birds began to build their nests, creating quite a din.
They chose some of the houses I had put up in the trees,
Where their little hungry chicks would shelter from the breeze.

It was in early April that
I got a great surprise.
I thought I had imagined it;
Could I believe my eyes?

Two ears popped out from underground;
then four, then six, then eight!
Exploring for the first time
to see what lay in wait.

Fox cubs tend to come outside
at this time of the year,
But then will go back underground
if they sense danger near.

So if you come across them while
they are clowning around,
Make sure to watch them from afar
and do not make a sound.

The days were getting longer and I had another guest.
My little hungry hedgehog friend was moving in her nest.
With hibernation over, tasty treats were on her mind.
She waited until darkness fell to see what she could find.

Small Beetles ran for cover, with earwigs close behind!

But Slugs and worms were out of luck and really in a bind.

She pounced and grabbed those juicy pests, the spikey little beast,

With starter, main course and dessert collected for her feast.

Did you know that hedgehogs love to go for walks at night?
They travel for a mile or more to find the food that's right.
And so it's up to all of us to help them on their quest,
To let them travel North to South, and then from East to West.

Like most gardens that we see, you'll have a fence or wall,
And this will stop them calling by (they are so very small).
So go and ask your neighbours if you can cut a hole,
And hopefully a hedgehog will decide to take a stroll.

April had run into May; our summer was ahead.
My thoughts had turned to planting out some flowers in their beds.

Sweet peas that I had sown in pots were first into the ground,
And as I placed the last one down, I heard a brand new sound.

"Tweet tweet,
Tweet tweet"

Up on high inside a house, white speckled eggs had hatched.
Tiny chicks peered to the sky, their hunger quite unmatched.
At first they were so very small and snuggled in their bed.
With heads kept down and bodies warm, they waited to be fed.

Their mood would change as soon as Mum or Dad dropped in with food.
Smalls mouths would shoot into the air; they were a noisy brood!
Beetles made a healthy snack, and caterpillars too,
While lots and lots of other bugs would end up in their stew.

June arrived and all the chicks were about three weeks old.
Full of feathers and quite big, they started to get bold.
A cheeky one looked up above and peeked her head outside,
And thought, "This would be a fine day to have a little glide."

"Careful now"

With long evenings and sunwashed days, the borders were in bloom.
Flowers rose up from the ground and didn't leave much room.
Lupins, sweet peas, sunflowers, all bathing in the heat,
Were joined by clumps of daisies in the grass beneath my feet.

Bees were dashing everywhere; their buzz a constant sound.
They harvested as much nectar as could be passed around.
Tables had been set for garden parties in July,
With smaller friends keeping a watch and revelling close by.

DID I MENTION THE BUTTERFLIES THAT VISITED MY HOME?
ACROSS THE TOPS OF FLOWER BEDS IS WHERE I SAW THEM ROAM.
I CAME ACROSS SMALL TORTOISESHELLS AND PEACOCKS EVERY DAY,
FLITTING HERE AND THERE IN A COLOURFUL DISPLAY.

August and September had them dotted everywhere.
Feasting on the nectar; there was plenty to share.
They fattened up their bellies as Summer came to a close,
And looked for hibernation spots where they could have a doze.

The days were getting shorter now; the summer said, "Goodbye!"
A slight chill could be felt with the sun lower in the sky.
Blackberries were ripe for picking by both young and old,
While leaves across the lofty trees were turning red and gold.

Blankets of these leaves covered the garden far and wide,
But ladybirds and other bugs just took it in their stride.
They foraged 'round for tasty treats to store in cubby holes,
And scooped up stocks of water before Winter took its toll.

Autumn is the perfect time for us to lend a hand.
We all can make a difference, as I'm sure you understand.
Piles of twigs and branches, or a plant pot on its side,
Will make the perfect refuge where these little bugs can hide.

The strangest thing occurred as October came to a close.
Leafless trees loomed overhead and scattered great shadows.
I saw what I thought must have been small ghosts fly here and there.
I'm not afraid to tell you now that I got quite a scare!

The mystery revealed itself throughout Halloween night.
The young birds from the neighbourhood flew in from left and right.
With costumes on, they visited the mums and dads up high
For berries, bugs and other treats before saying, "Goodbye."

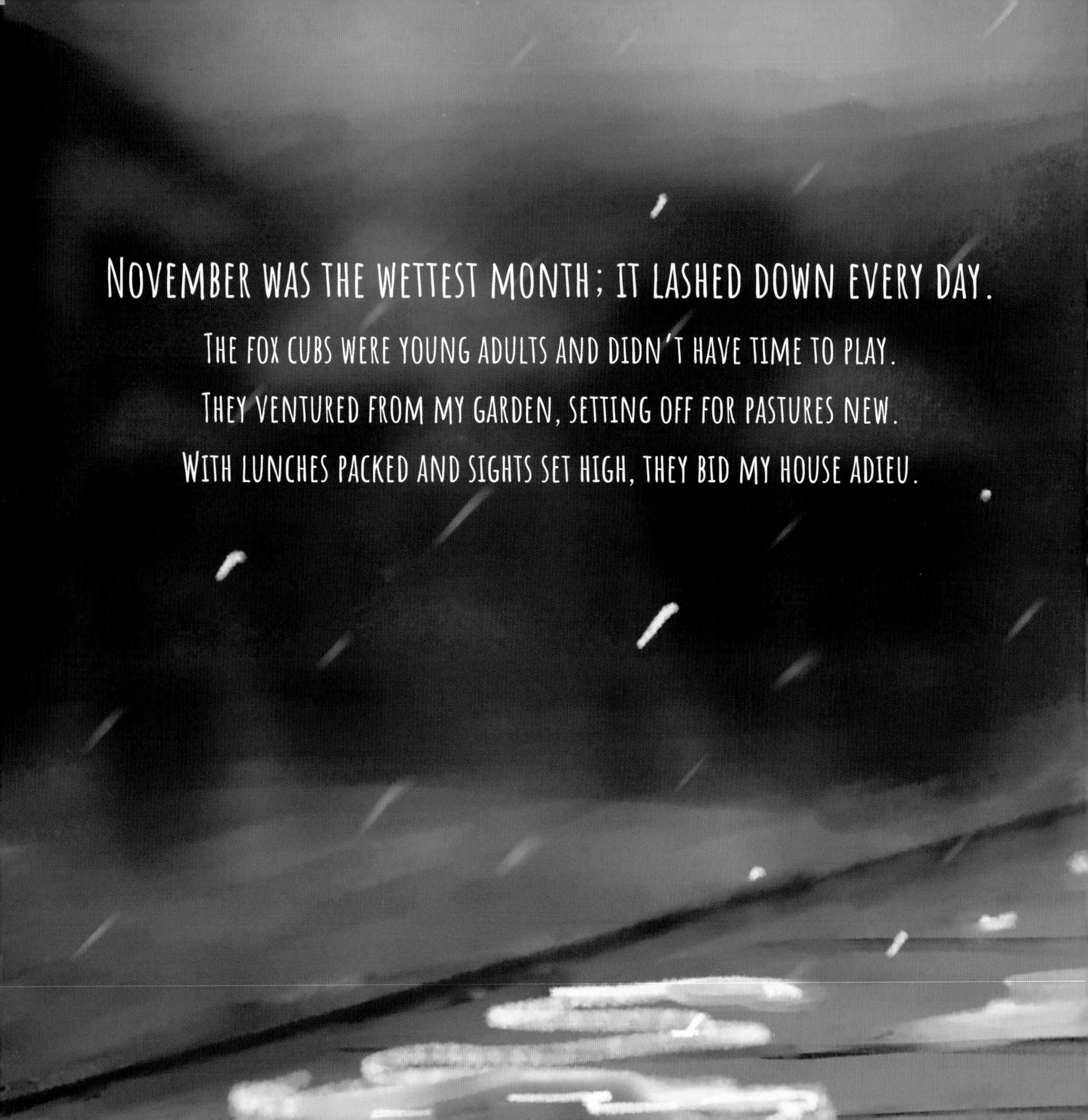

November was the wettest month; it lashed down every day.

The fox cubs were young adults and didn't have time to play.
They ventured from my garden, setting off for pastures new.
With lunches packed and sights set high, they bid my house adieu.

At last it was December and Yuletide was on the way.
The same old songs were played on the radio every day.
For once we had a white Christmas with snow across our lawn,
And a final few visitors that appeared around dawn.

You won't believe it but I saw three robins in that snow!

They laughed and sang and swapped their gifts, all wrapped up in a bow.

So keep an eye on your garden when Christmas comes around

Because, at this time of year, who knows what can be found.

I rang in the New Year with fireworks across the sky,
As joyful songs and laughter could be heard from homes nearby.
How lucky had I been to have such company all year,
That flew and crawled and hopped around my garden with great cheer.

And who should I spot resting underneath the bright full moon?
It was the friendly blackbird singing out his mellow tune.

"Should auld
acquaintance..."

Common Garden Visitors

Keep an eye out for them during the year

Honey Bees

Great Tit

Blue Tit

Peacock Butterflies

Small Tortoiseshell
Butterflies

Siskin

Printed in Cork, Ireland.

DonaghHourihan.com